Read-About® Geography

Chesapeake Bay

By Kelly Bennett

Subject Consultant
Lindsley Rice, Curator of Exhibitions
Chesapeake Bay Maritime Museum
Saint Michaels, Maryland

Reading Consultant
Cecilia Minden-Cupp, PhD
Former Director of the Language and Literacy Program
Harvard Graduate School of Education
Cambridge, Massachusetts

Children's Press®
A Division of Scholastic Inc.
New York   Toronto   London   Auckland   Sydney
Mexico City   New Delhi   Hong Kong
Danbury, Connecticut

Designer: Herman Adler Design
Photo Researcher: Caroline Anderson
The photo on the cover shows sea birds along the Chesapeake Bay.

Library of Congress Cataloging-in-Publication Data

Bennett, Kelly.
  Chesapeake Bay / by Kelly Bennett; subject consultant, Lindsley Rice;
reading consultant, Cecilia Minden-Cupp.
      p. cm. — (Rookie Read-About Geography)
  Includes index.
  ISBN 0-516-25032-9 (lib. bdg.)   0-516-29702-3 (pbk.)
  1. Chesapeake Bay (Md. and Va.)—Juvenile literature. 2. Chesapeake Bay
(Md. and Va.)—Geography—Juvenile literature. I. Title. II. Series.
  F187.C5B46 2006
  551.46'1347—dc22   2005021747

About 35,000 years ago,
a meteoroid crashed into
Earth. A meteoroid is a
rock from space.

Most meteoroids burn up as they fall through outer space. But others don't.

These meteoroids sometimes crash into Earth. The meteoroid that fell 35,000 years ago made a giant hole in the ground.

A hole caused by a meteoroid

A modern-day view of Chesapeake Bay

Glaciers once existed near the giant hole. A glacier is a slow-moving body of ice. Over time, the glaciers melted.

Rivers carried freshwater to the hole. Saltwater from the Atlantic Ocean poured in, too. The hole filled with water.

This hole and some of the rivers became the Chesapeake Bay.

The Chesapeake Bay is an estuary. An estuary is a place where freshwater and saltwater mix together.

A variety of plants and
animals live in the
Chesapeake Bay.

Those that can only live in freshwater stay near the rivers. Those that can only live in saltwater stay near the ocean.

Others, such as blue crabs, live throughout the bay.

The Chesapeake Bay is the largest estuary in the United States. Part of the bay is in Maryland. The other part is in Virginia.

Can you see where the Chesapeake Bay meets the Atlantic Ocean?

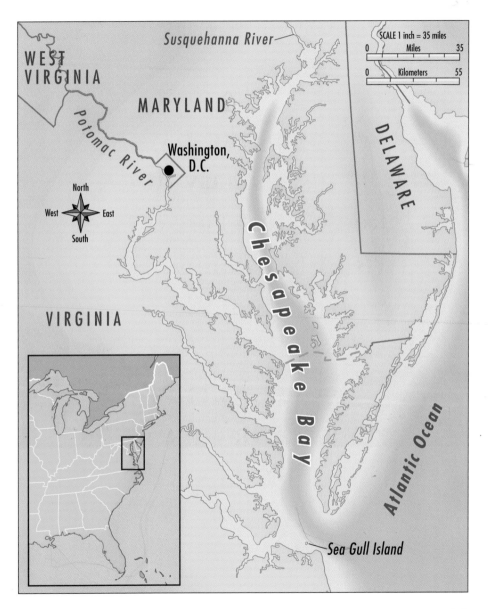

SCALE 1 inch = 35 miles

| 0 | Miles | 35 |

| 0 | Kilometers | 55 |

WEST
VIRGINIA

MARYLAND

Susquehanna River

Potomac River

Washington,
D.C.

North

West   East

South

VIRGINIA

DELAWARE

Chesapeake Bay

Atlantic Ocean

Sea Gull Island

13

The Susquehanna River

Many rivers carry water into the Chesapeake Bay. The Susquehanna River is the largest. About half of the freshwater in the bay comes from this river.

The Potomac River also carries water into the Chesapeake Bay. Ships on the Potomac haul goods between busy cities.

The ships travel downriver to the Chesapeake Bay. They then move into the Atlantic Ocean.

The Potomac River

The Bay Bridge crosses the Chesapeake Bay in Maryland.

The Bay Bridge is actually two bridges. Traffic on one bridge goes east. Traffic on the other bridge goes west.

Some people use the
Chesapeake Bay Bridge-
Tunnel to cross the bay
in Virginia. It is made
up of several bridges and
two tunnels.

Cars in the tunnels travel
underwater!

A view through the windshield of a car traveling in the
Chesapeake Bay Bridge-Tunnel

The Bay Bridge and one of the islands in the bay

These bridges and tunnels connect four islands. One of them is Sea Gull Island. People visit this island to fish and bird-watch.

Many people live around the Chesapeake Bay. Fishing and shipbuilding are important businesses there.

The Chesapeake Bay is a popular vacation spot, too.

Some people come to boat or fish. Others enjoy biking or hiking on trails near the bay. Many visitors like to swim or play in the sand.

Would you like to visit the
Chesapeake Bay?

What would you do first?

29

Words You Know

Bay Bridge

blue crabs

estuary

meteoroid

Potomac River

Susquehanna River

31

Index

About the Author

Kelly Bennett visited the Chesapeake Bay when she was a girl. She enjoys traveling with her family and writing about the places she visits. Kelly divides her time between Jakarta, Indonesia, and the United States.

Photo Credits

Photographs © 2006: Airphoto/Jim Wark: 22; Alamy Images/D.Y. Riess M.D.: 21; Corbis Images: 10, 30 top right (Lowell Georgia), 29 (Catherine Karnow), 17, 31 top right (Royalty-Free), 3, 31 top left (Sanford/Agliolo), 18, 25, 30 top left (Paul A. Souders); IPN Stock Images/Cameron Davidson: 9, 14, 30 bottom, 31 bottom; National Geographic Image Collection/Skip Brown: 26; Photo Researchers, NY: 5 (Francois Gohier), cover (USDA/Nature Source); Superstock, Inc./Ferrell McCollough: 6.

Map by Bob Italiano